INSIDE
HUMAN
BODY

By Dr. Aron Bruhn, MD

Illustrated by Joel Ito and Kathleen Kemly

STERLING

New York / London
www.sterlingpublishing.com/kids

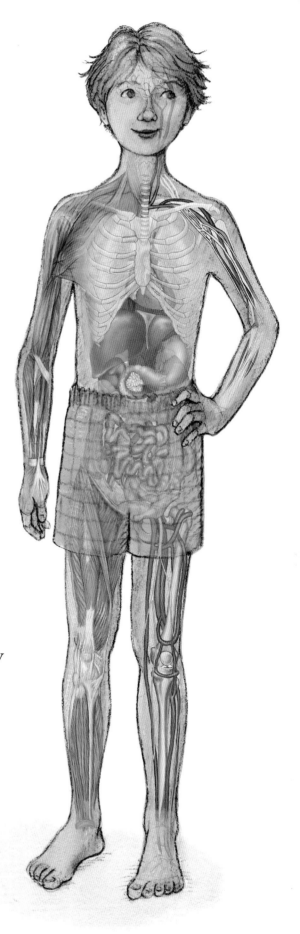

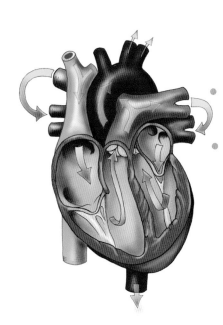

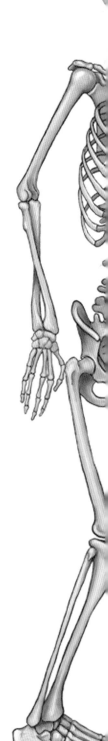

For my editor—the love of my life, my beautiful wife, Ashley.

STERLING and the distinctive Sterling logo are registered trademarks of
Sterling Publishing Co., Inc.

Library of Congress Cataloging-in-Publication Data

Bruhn, Aron, 1978-
  Inside the human body / by Aron Bruhn ; illustrations by Joel Ito and
Kathleen Kemly.
     p. cm.
  Includes index.
  ISBN 978-1-4027-7091-3 (hardcover) -- ISBN 978-1-4027-7779-0 (pbk.)
  1. Human body--Juvenile literature. I. Ito, Joel, ill. II. Kemly,
Kathleen Hadam, ill. III. Title.
  QP37.B887 2010
  612--dc22

                              2010002503

           2   4   6   8   10   9   7   5   3   1
                            05/10

Published by Sterling Publishing Co., Inc.
387 Park Avenue South, New York, NY 10016
© 2010 by Sterling Publishing Co., Inc.
Distributed in Canada by Sterling Publishing
c/o Canadian Manda Group, 165 Dufferin Street
Toronto, Ontario, Canada M6K 3H6
Distributed in the United Kingdom by GMC Distribution Services
Castle Place, 166 High Street, Lewes, East Sussex, England BN7 1XU
Distributed in Australia by Capricorn Link (Australia) Pty. Ltd.
P.O. Box 704, Windsor, NSW 2756, Australia

Design by Ye Huang & Han Xu

Front cover photograph © Maxine Hall/CORBIS
Cover illustration by Joel Ito and Kathleen Kemly

Sterling ISBN 978-1-4027-7091-3 (hardcover)
Sterling ISBN 978-1-4027-7779-0 (paperback)

For information about custom editions, special sales, premium and
corporate purchases, please contact Sterling Special Sales Department
at 800-805-5489 or specialsales@sterlingpublishing.com.

Look Inside!

YOUR BODY IS AN AMAZING THING. IT ALLOWS YOU TO DO everything from running to reading. It heals itself when injured and increases twenty times in size from when you are born to when you are an adult. You can experience the world through five different senses, learn new things, and play games. You can do all these wonderful things because of all the amazing systems you have inside your body.

A cell is the smallest living unit—but it is filled with important stuff! Inside each cell is a set of *organelles*: tiny structures designed to help the cell accomplish its goal. The biggest structure of them all is the *nucleus*. The nucleus contains two copies of each of your twenty-three *chromosomes* (one copy from your mother and one from your father). These chromosomes contain the blueprints or instructions to make you *you*. The instructions are called *DNA (deoxyribonucleic acids).*

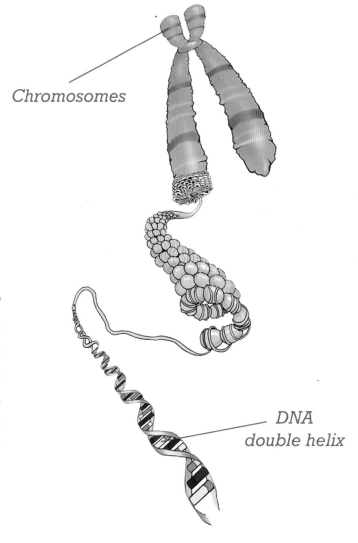

Chromosomes

DNA double helix

Every organ in your body is made up of **CELLS** and functions because of cells. Depending on the organ, cells can clean blood, help with digestion, allow fresh oxygen to enter your body, move muscles, and even allow you to think—and to read this book!

Your skin and everything underneath it make up a **COMPLEX SYSTEM** of different organs that are each doing a unique task to help make you work.

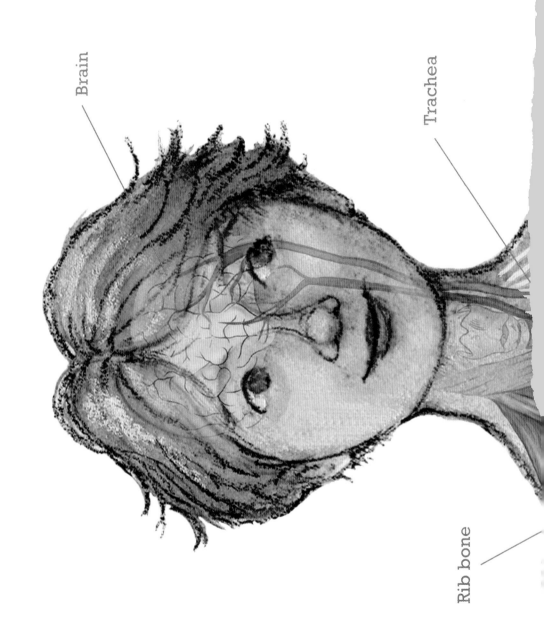

Brain

Trachea

Rib bone

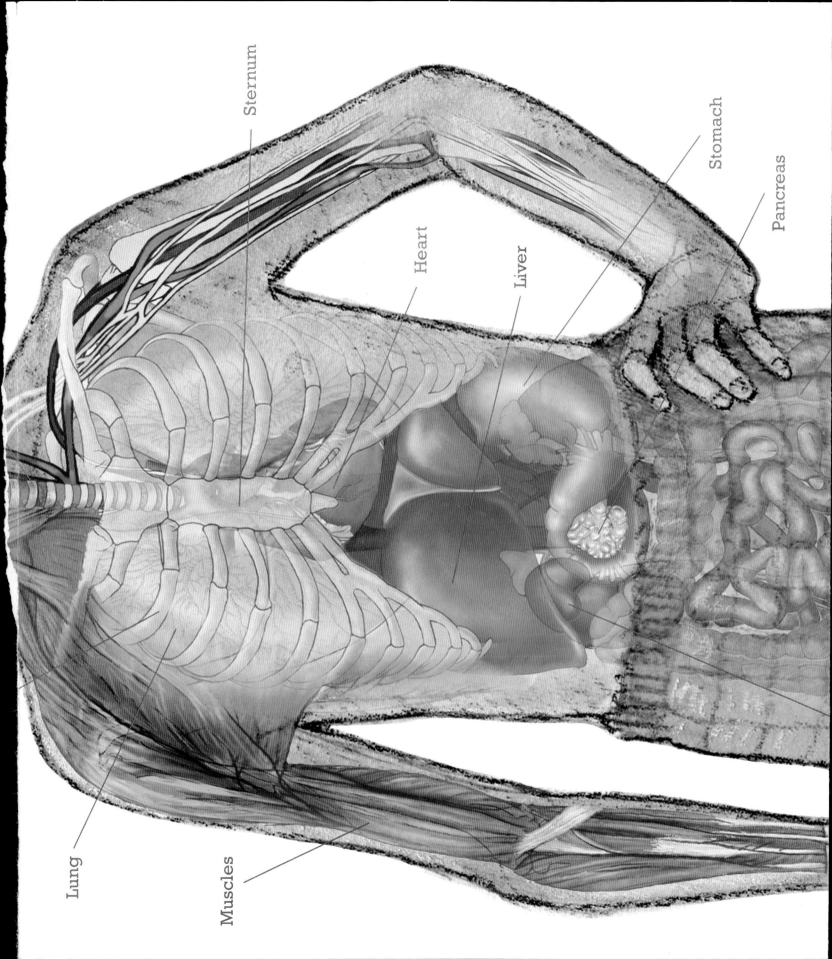

Contents

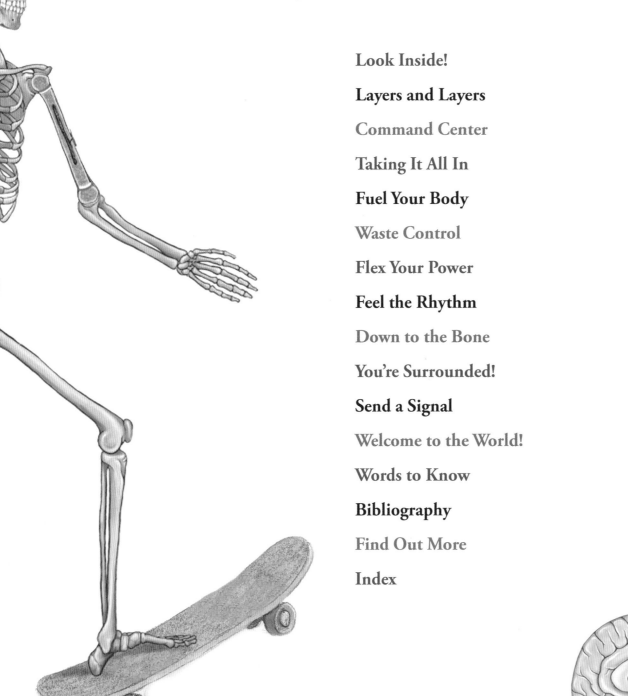

Layers and Layers

YOUR SKIN PLAYS AN IMPORTANT ROLE IN YOUR HEALTH. It not only protects you from germs but also helps to regulate your temperature, senses the environment around you, and prevents you from getting soaking wet (like a sponge) or totally dried out (like beef jerky).

The outer most layer of your skin, called the *epidermis*, is where all skin cells begin. The cells at the base of the epidermis never move but instead constantly divide and make copies of themselves. These copies flatten like pancakes and rise to the surface. When all of these cells are stacked together, they form the epidermis.

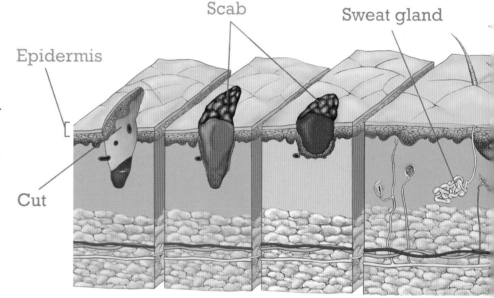

Scab

Sweat gland

Epidermis

Cut

When you cut yourself, a blood clot (scab) forms to fill in the gap until skin cells can grow into the cut and heal it.

Your **SKIN** is actually the largest organ in your whole body. If you were to lay out an adult's skin, it could cover a twin bed!

How Old is Your Skin?

It takes about thirty-five days for a cell to make the journey from the base of the epidermis to the top of your skin. That means that almost every month you get a whole new coat of skin!

?

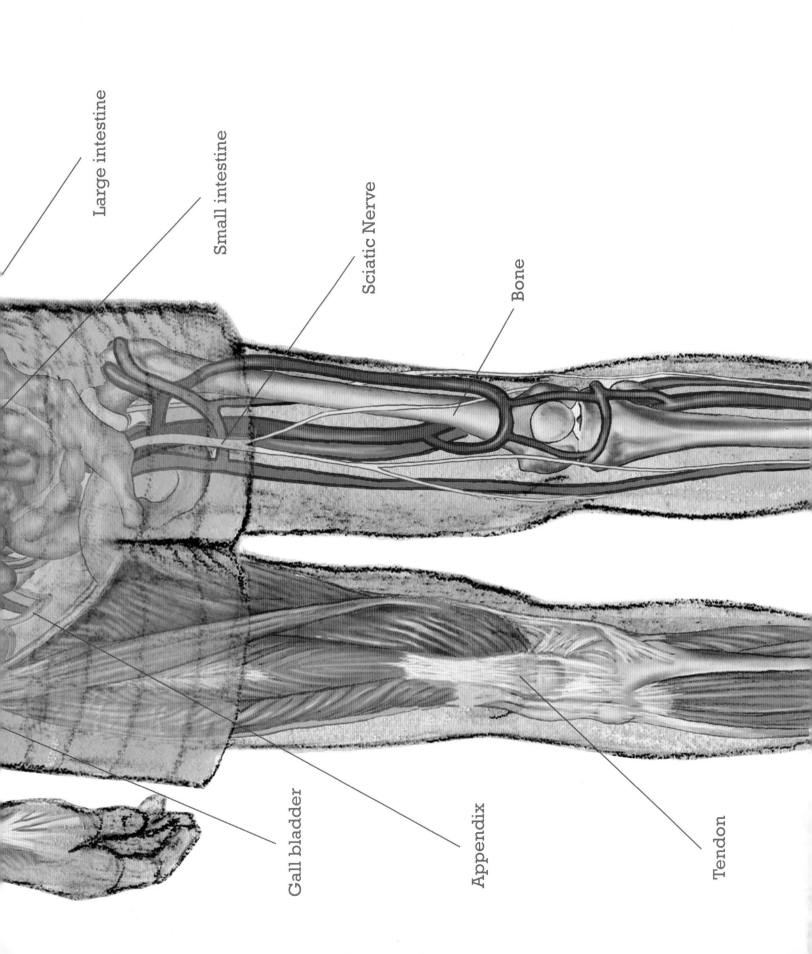

Large intestine

Small intestine

Sciatic Nerve

Bone

Gall bladder

Appendix

Tendon

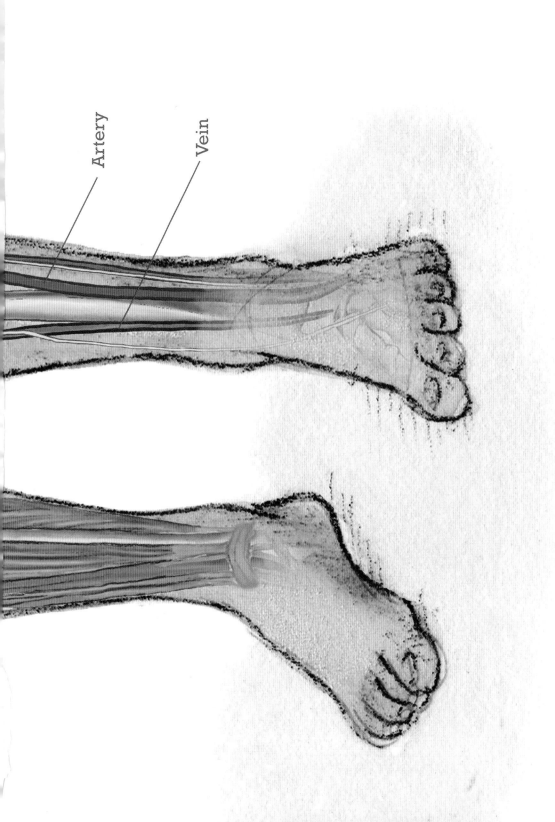

Artery

Vein

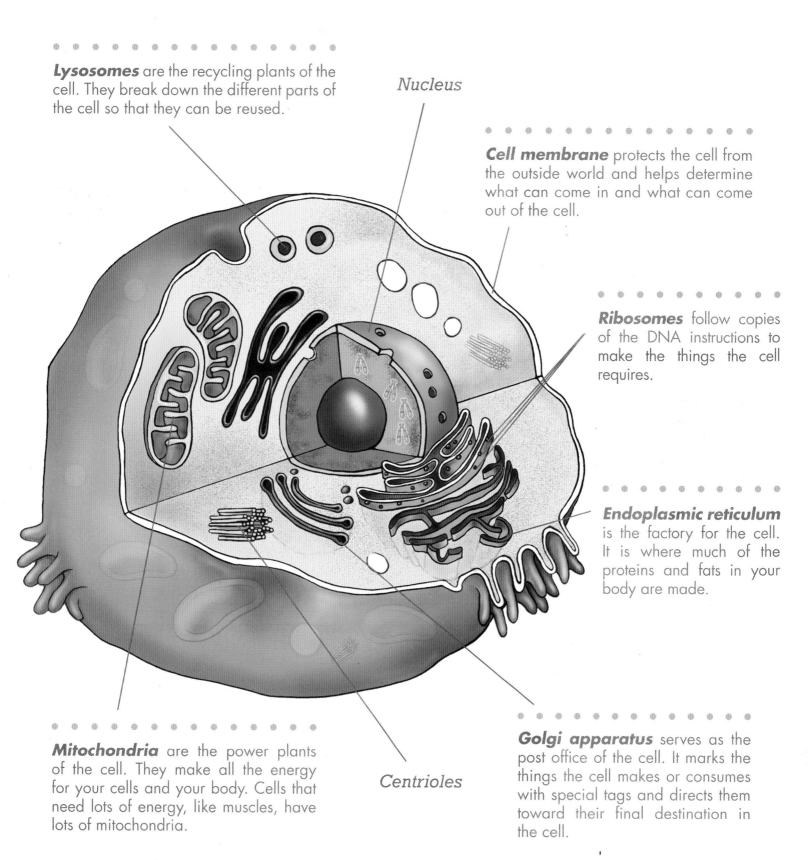

Lysosomes are the recycling plants of the cell. They break down the different parts of the cell so that they can be reused.

Nucleus

Cell membrane protects the cell from the outside world and helps determine what can come in and what can come out of the cell.

Ribosomes follow copies of the DNA instructions to make the things the cell requires.

Endoplasmic reticulum is the factory for the cell. It is where much of the proteins and fats in your body are made.

Mitochondria are the power plants of the cell. They make all the energy for your cells and your body. Cells that need lots of energy, like muscles, have lots of mitochondria.

Centrioles

Golgi apparatus serves as the post office of the cell. It marks the things the cell makes or consumes with special tags and directs them toward their final destination in the cell.

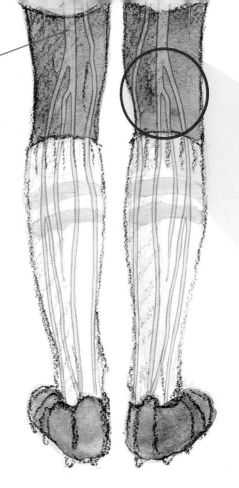

Sciatic nerve

NERVES run in both directions. While nerve signals run down to make your muscles contract so you can kick a ball, they also send signals up to tell you that your foot hit the ball.

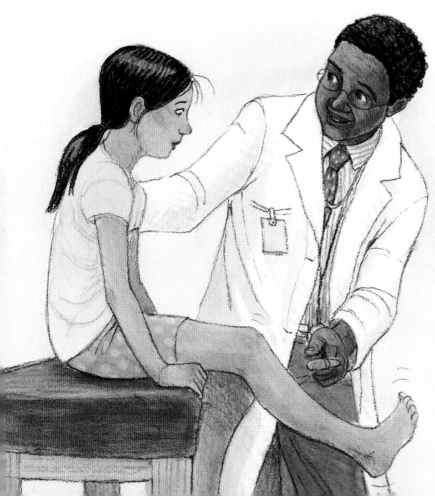

REFLEXES are what the doctor tests when using a mallet on your knee to make you kick.

Don't Forget Sunscreen!

Sometimes things in the skin go wrong. But while you can't see your other organs, the problems that develop in the skin are in plain sight. When your skin cells get damaged from too much sun, you might see a sunburn or a blister as your skin attempts to heal itself. If this happens too often, the skin cells might begin reproducing themselves uncontrollably, causing skin cancer, the most serious of which is melanoma.

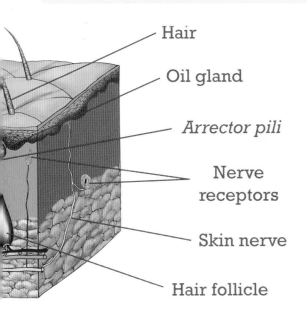

- Hair
- Oil gland
- *Arrector pili*
- Nerve receptors
- Skin nerve
- Hair follicle

Why Freckles?

Melanocytes are tiny cells that are there to protect you. When they sense you are being exposed to ultraviolet light from the sun, they send *melanin* (a dark pigment) up skinny arm-like structures to act as minisunshades for the cells of your skin. The melanin is what makes you tan. Dark-skinned individuals are born with more active melanocytes than light-skinned individuals. Freckles are just clusters of melanin that cause the skin in an area to be darker.

When your skin is **BRUISED**, blood vessels leak blood; and your skin appears dark blue, just like the skin near your veins.

Uh-Oh...

Oil glands are important for keeping your skin water repellant and soft. But when oil glands become clogged, bacteria on your skin can get into the blocked gland and form a small infection called a pimple.

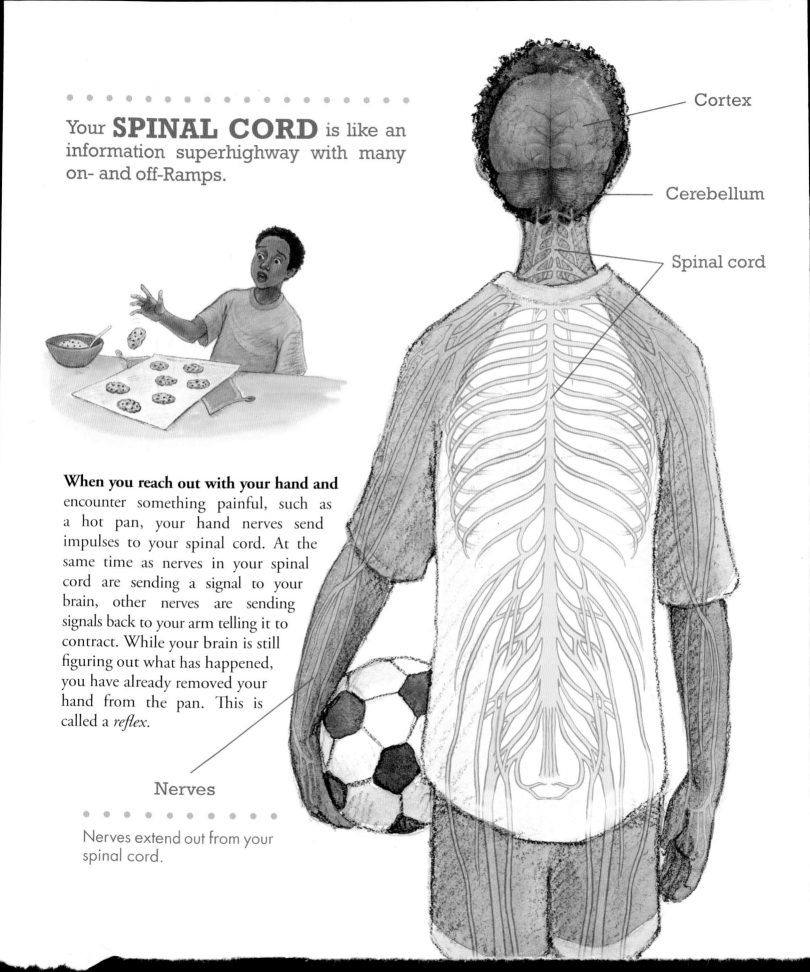

Your **SPINAL CORD** is like an information superhighway with many on- and off-Ramps.

Cortex

Cerebellum

Spinal cord

When you reach out with your hand and encounter something painful, such as a hot pan, your hand nerves send impulses to your spinal cord. At the same time as nerves in your spinal cord are sending a signal to your brain, other nerves are sending signals back to your arm telling it to contract. While your brain is still figuring out what has happened, you have already removed your hand from the pan. This is called a *reflex*.

Nerves

Nerves extend out from your spinal cord.

Command Center

ALL OF YOUR THOUGHTS, SENSATIONS, AND MOVEMENTS are partly or fully controlled by your nervous system, which is made up of two parts: Your *central nervous system* includes your brain and your spinal cord. Your *peripheral nervous system* is made up of nerves extending from your spinal cord into your arms and legs.

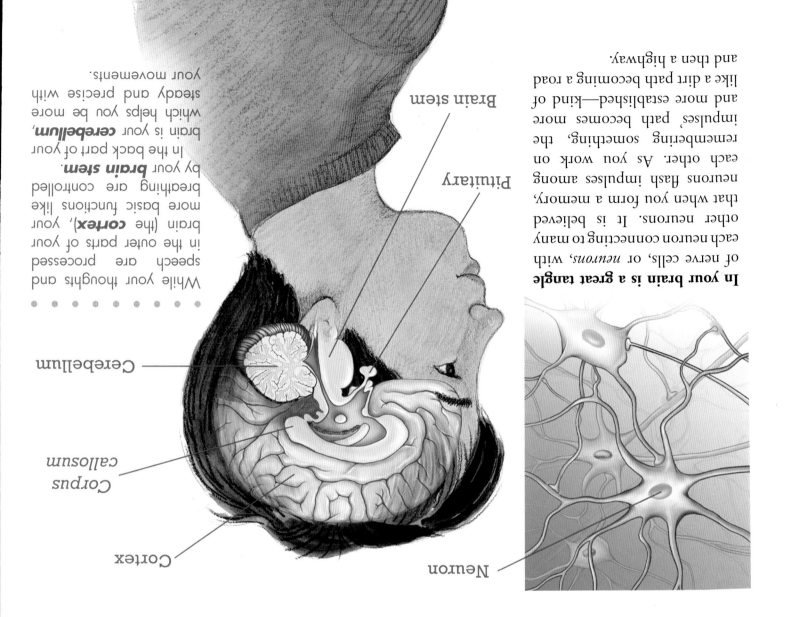

Cerebellum

Corpus callosum

Cortex

Brain stem

Pituitary

Neuron

In your brain is a great tangle of nerve cells, or *neurons*, with each neuron connecting to many other neurons. It is believed that when you form a memory, neurons flash impulses among each other. As you work on remembering something, the impulses' path becomes more and more established—kind of like a dirt path becoming a road and then a highway.

While your thoughts and speech are processed in the outer parts of your brain (the **cortex**), your more basic functions like breathing are controlled by your **brain stem**. In the back part of your brain is your **cerebellum,** which helps you be more steady and precise with your movements.

Taking It All In

THERE ARE FIVE SENSES YOU USE TO UNDERSTAND the world around you. Your body has several specialized organs that allow you to see, taste, hear, touch, and smell the environment around you.

Hearing

Your ears are designed to help convert vibrations into sound. Your ears sense vibrations in the air and signal the brain.

Smelling

Noses come in all shapes and sizes, but they all help us breathe, and they house the nerves responsible for our sense of smell.

Hearing: Listen Up!

Your ear can be divided into three parts: the outer, middle, and inner ear. The outer ear, the part you can see in the mirror, is designed to channel sound waves into the ear canal (your middle ear) to help you hear. Sound waves travel inside your middle ear to the *tympanic membrane*, or eardrum, a thin layer of tissue that vibrates as sound waves hit it. That vibration is passed on to tiny ear bones in the inner ear, which cause fluid in the *cochlea* to ripple. When tiny hairs inside your cochlea get disturbed by the rippling, they send a nerve impulse to your brain, which you interpret as a sound.

Check It Out!

Your inner ear holds the smallest bones in your body: the *malleus*, the *stapes*, and the *incus*. The stapes is about the size of Abe Lincoln's ear on the penny!

Can You Clear Your Ears?

Your eardrum keeps a pocket of trapped air behind it. When you change altitude quickly, as you do in a plane, the pocket of air can expand or contract and place pressure on your eardrum (which can be really uncomfortable). A tube, called the *eustachian tube*, connects your ear to your mouth. When you yawn to "clear your ears," the tube opens and relieves the pressure.

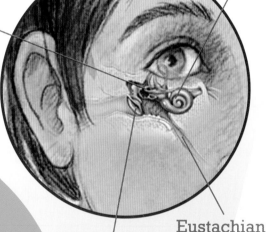

Cochlea

Semicircular canals

Eustachian tube

Tympanic membrane

Smelling: Take A Whiff!

At the top of the nasal passage are the cells responsible for your sense of smell. In fact, it's your nose more than your tongue that tells you the flavor of your food. While your tongue can sense only five tastes, your nose can smell around ten thousand different smells! Specialized cells in your nose sense small molecules in the air and then send signals all over your brain to trigger memories, hunger, or simple recognition of what you smell.

Your nose does more than just smell: it works to warm and humidify air before it enters your lungs, and it prvents dust and germs from getting too deep into your body. Although your nostrils are relatively small, they open up into larger structures call *turbinates* and *sinuses,* which are covered with mucus (sometimes called snot). When dust or germs hit the mucus, they get stuck and are eventually removed from your body.

Sinuses

Turbinates

Eustachian tube

Sound Different?

Have you ever noticed that your voice changes when you get a cold? That is partly because your airways get filled with mucus. This changes the airflow when you speak, the same way pressing the keys on a trumpet changes its sound.

Fun Fact!

Your nose, like your ear, is largely made up of cartilage—which is the same substance that makes up a shark's skeleton.

Ever wonder why your **NOSE** runs when you cry? Your *nasolacrimal duct* carries tear fluid from the eye into the nose.

Sore Throat?

When you have a cold, you produce extra mucus that can help you get rid of the virus. The excess mucus often runs down the back of your throat, which can irritate it, and cause a sore throat.

Making Connections

In the peripheral nervous system, nerve cells transfer information among each other in the form of electrical impulses through long fibers called *axons*. Each axon is insulated by a *Schwann cell*, which is wrapped around the axon (much like rubber is wrapped around an electrical wire). Schwann cells ensure that the electrical impulse moves quickly and that the information is only transmitted at the very end of the nerve.

At the nerve's end is something called a *synapse*. At the synapse, a message is transmitted from the nerve, telling another cell that an action needs to be taken. In the case of a muscle, that action is a contraction. When you want your leg to move so that you can kick a ball, your brain sends an electrical impulse down the axon to the synapse, where the signal is received. Your muscle then contracts, and your leg moves.

Neuron

Axon

Synapse

Schwann cell   Muscle

Homunculus Man

This funny-looking person is called a *homunculus*. He represents how much of your brain is devoted to each part of your body. Certain parts of your brain are responsible for certain parts of your body, but this distribution is not equal. Look at how much more of your brain is devoted to controlling your hands and mouth than to working your elbows and feet! You can write, play an instrument, draw, play video games, and do many wonderfully complex things with your hands! But all you can really do with your elbow is bend it.

Did You Know?

The right half of your brain controls the left side of your body, and the left half controls the right side.

?

Seeing

Humans' eyes allow for pretty good color vision, especially when compared with a dog's. But a hawk's vision is eight times sharper than ours.

Touching

Skin houses the nerve structures responsible for your sense of touch. Special nerve structures sense pressure, while others sense temperature and pain.

Tasting

Taste is a big part of why we like food. But it turns out that the tongue contributes a lot less to taste than you may think!

21

Tasting: Savor the Flavor!

Taste buds—small structures on your tongue—hold cells that are capable of sensing one of five different flavors: sweet, salty, bitter, sour, or umami (found in soy sauce). All five flavors can be tasted by cells that are distributed all over your tongue and that are even in the back and on the roof of your mouth.

Spicy is your tongue's perception of pain. That's why it feels like it's burning.

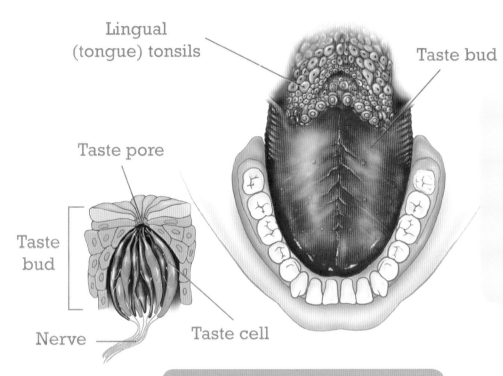

Lingual (tongue) tonsils

Taste bud

Taste pore

Taste bud

Nerve

Taste cell

Try It!

Your tongue is actually a very large muscle. Unlike other muscles, which have a fairly limited range of motion, your tongue can twist and turn in any number of ways. This range of motion is essential for you to talk. Try talking while holding your tongue. Can you still speak clearly?

Ewww... Gross!

Your teeth are covered with bacteria that eat all the same foods that you eat. These bacteria can build up, forming huge colonies that we call plaque. You can get rid of the plaque by brushing and flossing your teeth, and it's important that you do! Waste products from the bacteria (bacterial poop!) can dissolve your teeth and cause cavities.

Are Teeth Alive?

Yes! The part of the tooth that you see in your mouth is only the tip. Beneath your gums sits the *pulp* of the tooth, where nerves and blood vessels are working to keep the tooth alive.

?

Touching: Feel That? Check out pages 13-14 to learn more about your sense of touch!

Seeing: Look Around!

Your eyes let you see the world around you. Light rays bounce off an object and then travel through the outermost layer of your eye, the *cornea*, which starts to focus an image of that object. Next, light passes through your lens. The lens sharpens the focus of the image, using tiny muscles. The light is focused onto the *retina*, where the image appears like a projected movie, only upside down. Your amazing brain flips the image automatically so you still see right side up!

If you try to look at something very close to your nose, your **EYES** cross. We judge distance in part by sensing how much our eyes are crossed.

People who need glasses have muscles that are either too tight or too loose to allow the lens to focus well.

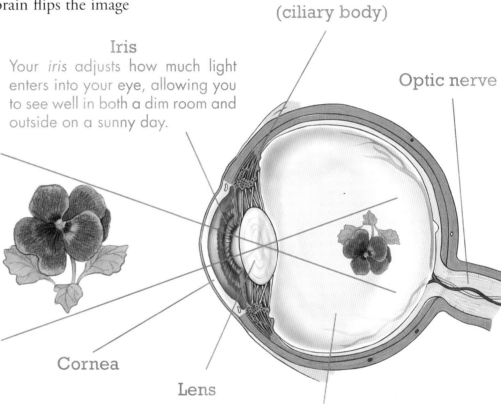

Muscle (ciliary body)

Optic nerve

Iris

Your *iris* adjusts how much light enters into your eye, allowing you to see well in both a dim room and outside on a sunny day.

Cornea

Lens

Retina

Your *retina* houses light sensitive cells called *cones* and *rods*. Cones see in color, while rods see only in black and white. Cones need lots of light, but rods can work well even in dim light. This is why seeing color in dim light, such as by moonlight, is so difficult.

Each of the rods and cones connects to a nerve fiber. These nerve fibers meet to form your *optic nerve*. Where the optic nerve forms on the retina, there are no cones or rods, causing a blind spot.

Find Your Blind Spot!

Your brain compensates for the blind spot by guessing, but you can find your blind spot if you trick your brain. Look at the X on the bottom of the page but pay attention to the black circle. Next, covering your right eye, hold the book at arm's length and slowly bring it closer to your face. The circle should disappear. You've found your blind spot!

●   ✗

Fuel Your Body

WHAT YOU EAT HELPS YOU GROW AND ALLOWS YOUR organs to work. When you eat, nutrients from your meal are broken down by your digestive organs so that your body can absorb them and use them to make new muscles, bones, other tissues, and energy.

As Big as a Tennis Court!

Your intestine is around twenty-five feet long, folded many times over, and is designed for absorption. On its surface are very tiny finger-like extensions (villi), and on each tiny finger there are microscopic fingers (microvilli). All those fingers increase the surface area of the intestine to give the food more places where it can be absorbed. All in all, your intestine has the same amount of surface as a tennis court!

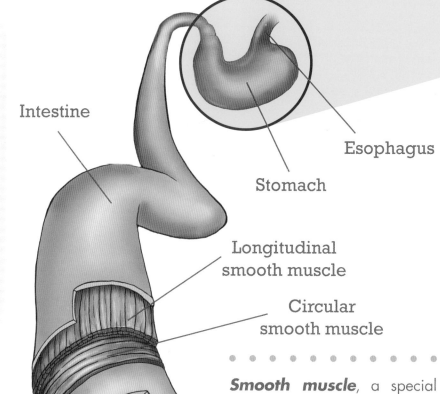

Intestine

Esophagus

Stomach

Longitudinal smooth muscle

Circular smooth muscle

Villi

Intestinal folds

Smooth muscle, a special type of muscle that almost never gets tired, surrounds your digestive tract. It is arranged in two main layers, and each layer can squeeze independently. These layers mix up the broken-down food and move it down the tract.

Fuel Your Body

WHAT YOU EAT HELPS YOU GROW AND ALLOWS YOUR organs to work. When you eat, nutrients from your meal are broken down by your digestive organs so that your body can absorb them and use them to make new muscles, bones, other tissues, and energy.

As Big as a Tennis Court!

Your intestine is around twenty-five feet long, folded many times over, and is designed for absorption. On its surface are very tiny finger-like extensions (villi), and on each tiny finger there are microscopic fingers (microvilli). All those fingers increase the surface area of the intestine to give the food more places where it can be absorbed. All in all, your intestine has the same amount of surface as a tennis court!

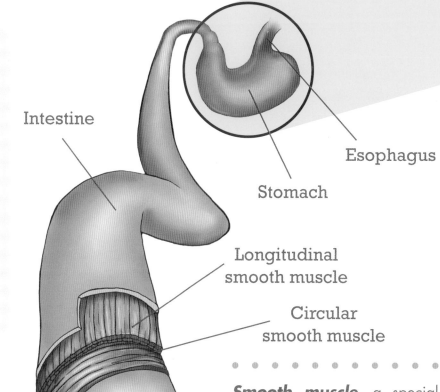

Intestine

Esophagus

Stomach

Longitudinal smooth muscle

Circular smooth muscle

Villi

Intestinal folds

Smooth muscle, a special type of muscle that almost never gets tired, surrounds your digestive tract. It is arranged in two main layers, and each layer can squeeze independently. These layers mix up the broken-down food and move it down the tract.

Seeing: Look Around!

Your eyes let you see the world around you. Light rays bounce off an object and then travel through the outermost layer of your eye, the *cornea*, which starts to focus an image of that object. Next, light passes through your lens. The lens sharpens the focus of the image, using tiny muscles. The light is focused onto the *retina*, where the image appears like a projected movie, only upside down. Your amazing brain flips the image automatically so you still see right side up!

If you try to look at something very close to your nose, your **EYES** cross. We judge distance in part by sensing how much our eyes are crossed.

People who need glasses have muscles that are either too tight or too loose to allow the lens to focus well.

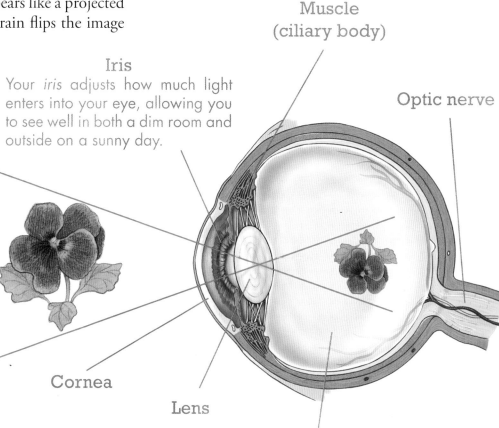

Muscle (ciliary body)

Optic nerve

Iris
Your *iris* adjusts how much light enters into your eye, allowing you to see well in both a dim room and outside on a sunny day.

Cornea

Lens

Retina
Your *retina* houses light sensitive cells called *cones* and *rods*. Cones see in color, while rods see only in black and white. Cones need lots of light, but rods can work well even in dim light. This is why seeing color in dim light, such as by moonlight, is so difficult.

Each of the rods and cones connects to a nerve fiber. These nerve fibers meet to form your *optic nerve*. Where the optic nerve forms on the retina, there are no cones or rods, causing a blind spot.

Find Your Blind Spot!

Your brain compensates for the blind spot by guessing, but you can find your blind spot if you trick your brain. Look at the X on the bottom of the page but pay attention to the black circle. Next, covering your right eye, hold the book at arm's length and slowly bring it closer to your face. The circle should disappear. You've found your blind spot!

●   ✕

Chew and Swallow

Digestion starts in your mouth with simple chewing. When you chew, you break your food into much smaller pieces. *Saliva* in your mouth is incorporated into the food as your tongue mashes and mixes the broken pieces. Your tongue groups a small clump of food together and pushes it down into your *esophagus*. The esophagus is essentially a tube that connects your mouth with your stomach.

Fats

• •

FOOD falls into three categories: fats, proteins, and carbohydrates.

Proteins

Next . . .

Food travels from your mouth down through your esophagus into your abdomen. But the food doesn't just fall down the hole; it is pushed down during a series of wave-like squeezes, called *peristalsis*. When food gets to the end of your esophagus, a tight circular muscle, called a *sphincter*, opens to allow food to pass into your stomach—and then closes again to ensure that the food does not come back out.

Give it a try!

Your saliva contains a protein called *amylase*, which converts complex sugars into simple ones. Although complex sugars don't taste sweet, simple ones do. In fact, if you take a piece of a soda cracker (a complex sugar) and let it dissolve really slowly in your mouth, the amylase converts it so it starts to taste sweet!

Carbohydrates

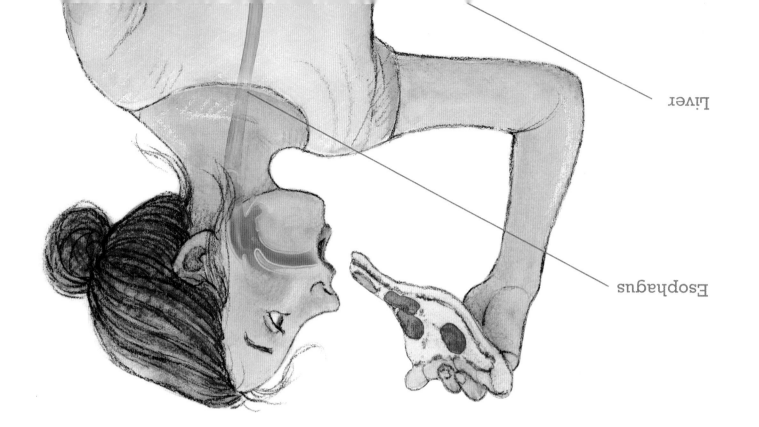

Liver

Esophagus

Inside Your Stomach

Your stomach gently squeezes the food inside it, mixing it with acid, and after a sufficient amount of time has passed, the food is squeezed through another sphincter into your *small intestine.*

How Strong?

Your stomach juice has one million times more acid than tap water and is strong enough to corrode metal! The acid not only aids in digestion but also kills many bacteria, some of which could cause infections. Your stomach is protected from its own acid by a layer of mucus.

Digestion

Your small intestine is where most of digestion occurs. The *pancreas* and your *gall bladder* empty their juices into the small intestine. While your pancreas makes *digestive enzymes* that break down proteins and carbohydrates, your gall bladder stores *bile,* a substance made in your liver that helps digest fat. Once all the food is broken down, it is absorbed by the intestine and distributed to your body where it can be used to fuel your activities or to help you grow.

Once food leaves the small intestine, it enters the *large intestine.* This is where most of the liquid you drink is absorbed. Any food not absorbed by your body leaves your body as waste (poop).

Your **DIGESTIVE TRACT** is essentially a long tube running from your mouth to your rectum. But lots of organs in between help digest your food.

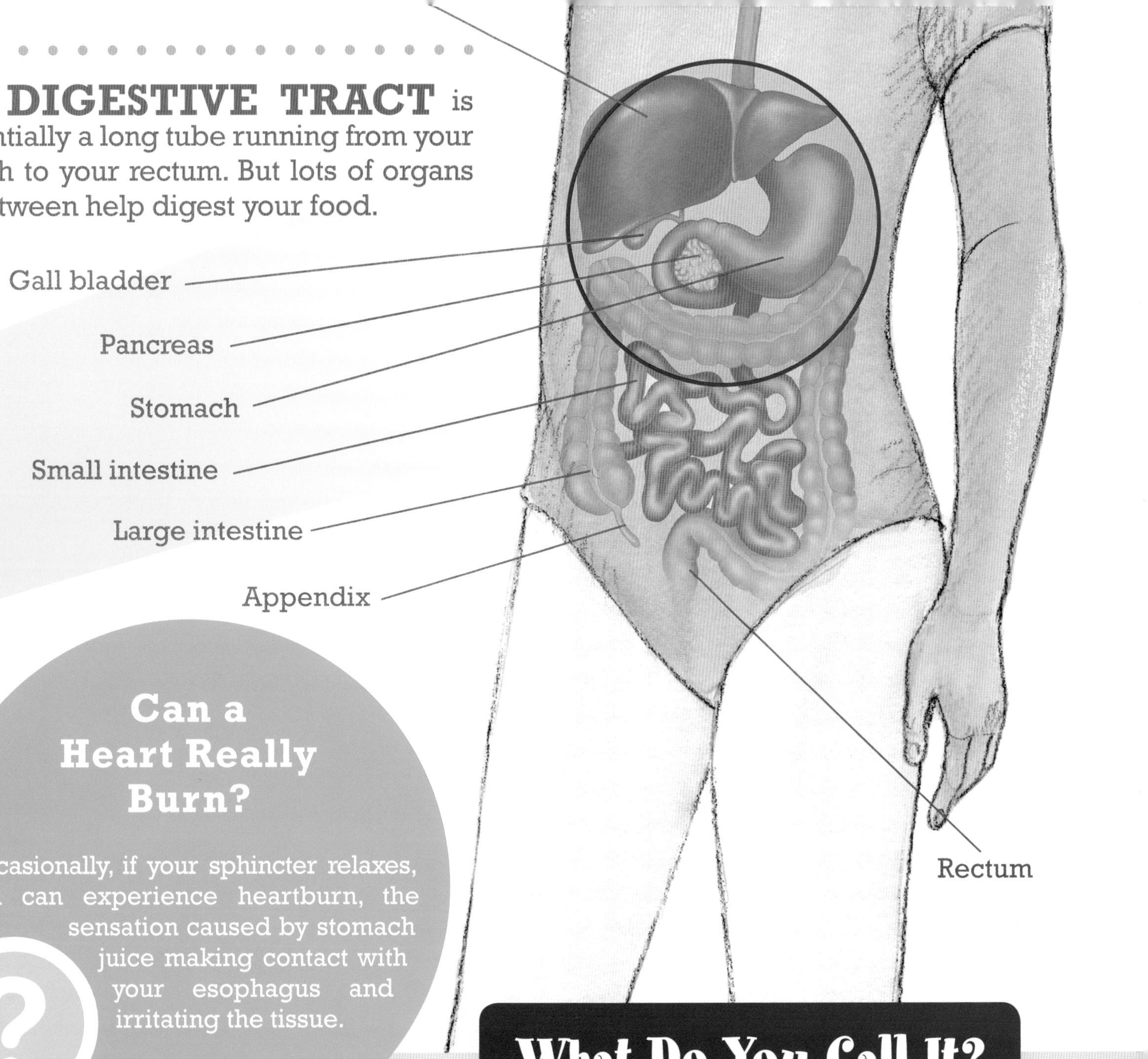

Gall bladder

Pancreas

Stomach

Small intestine

Large intestine

Appendix

Rectum

Can a Heart Really Burn?

Occasionally, if your sphincter relaxes, you can experience heartburn, the sensation caused by stomach juice making contact with your esophagus and irritating the tissue.

?

What Do You Call It?

Your large intestine is home to bacteria that live naturally in the body. These bacteria digest the parts of the food that you cannot digest, and when they do, they make gas. When the gas makes it way all the way to your *rectum* and out your body, doctors call it *flatus*, (although you may know it as farting). When you eat food that you cannot fully digest, like beans, the bacteria make more gas. These bacteria also make vitamin K and can protect you from other types of illness-causing bacteria.

Waste Control

AS YOU GO ABOUT YOUR DAY, YOUR BODY MAKES COMPOUNDS that have to be eliminated from your system. This task falls in part to your kidneys. Your kidneys act like filters for your blood: waste and salt are washed away into *urine* (pee) while the good things in the blood are kept in your blood.

Making Urine

Urine production occurs in a tiny structure called a *nephron*—a long, narrow tube in your kidney. Nephrons are so small that each kidney has almost one million nephrons! At the start of the nephron, the blood vessels divide into a tiny tangle of *capillaries* called *Bowman's capsule*. These capillaries are very leaky and allow water, salts, and other waste to filter out of your blood and into the nephron. The waste then drains down the collecting ducts into your *renal pelvis*, where it can be called urine. The clean blood goes back to your heart.

The more liquid you drink, the more water your kidneys can use to wash your blood, and your urine gets clear. The less water you drink, the more your kidneys have to conserve water in your body, resulting in very concentrated, yellow urine.

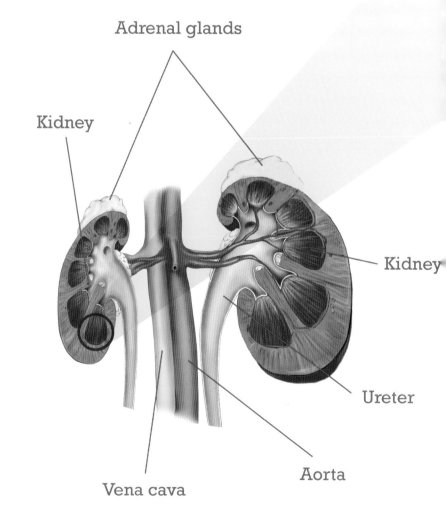

Adrenal glands

Kidney

Kidney

Ureter

Aorta

Vena cava

Flex Your Power

THERE ARE THREE DIFFERENT TYPES OF MUSCLES IN your body: *cardiac*, *smooth*, and *skeletal*. Smooth muscle is found in your digestive organs, while cardiac muscle is found only in your heart, But skeletal muscle makes up what most of us think of as muscle (the kind you flex when you curl your arm). Skeletal muscle is unique in that it is under conscious control—you can control its motion.

The muscles in your face connect directly to your skin, pulling your skin this way and that. This allows you to frown, smile, or squint your eyes— among other things.

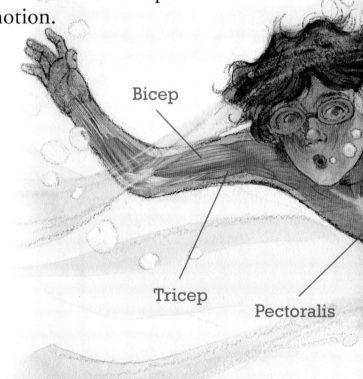

Bicep

Tricep

Pectoralis

Your **HANDS** are very important, and you have the muscles to prove it! You have fifteen muscles in each forearm that help you control the motion in your hands, plus another ten muscles in each hand. That's twenty-five muscles for just one hand!

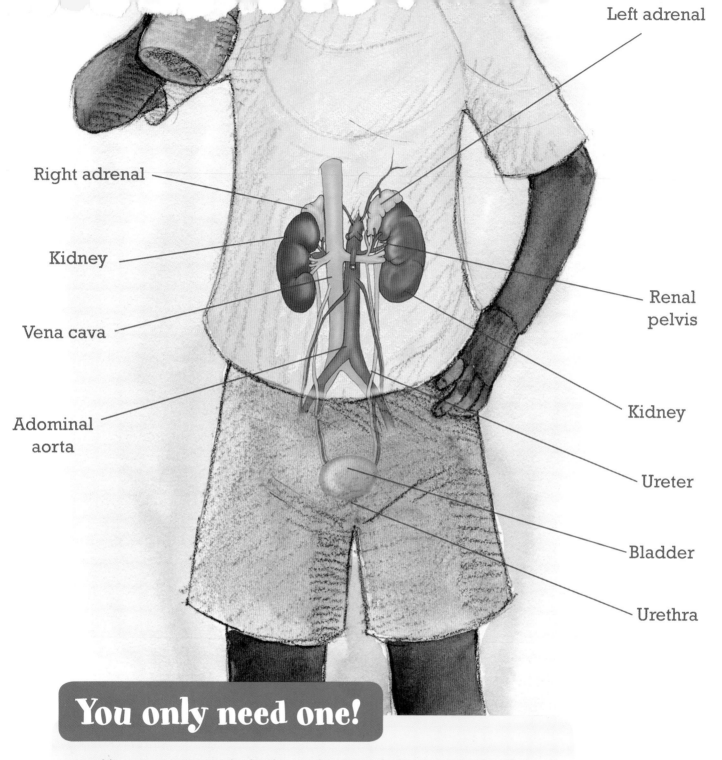

Left adrenal

Right adrenal

Kidney

Vena cava

Adominal aorta

Renal pelvis

Kidney

Ureter

Bladder

Urethra

You only need one!

Unlike most organs in the body, you have two kidneys—but even if one kidney is damaged or removed, your other kidney can still do its job, getting rid of any excess fluid and waste from your blood. That means that someone can donate one of his or her kidneys to be transplanted into someone else who has two failed kidneys.

Esophagus

Did You Know?

Unlike feces (poop), urine comes out of the body sterile, meaning that it has no bacteria growing in it at all.

After **URINE** is formed, it collects in the pelvis of the kidney. From there it is transferred down the ureter and into the bladder.

Your body is almost two thirds water. An adult requires one to two liters of water a day to maintain all vital body functions. You have a built-in regulation system to help make sure you get enough fluid—**THIRST!**

Bowman's capsule

Collecting duct

May I Be Excused?

Although your kidneys drip urine all the time, your bladder allows you to store the urine until it is more convenient to empty it. (Thank goodness!) When your bladder starts to get stretched, it sends signals to your brain that you need go to the bathroom. In response, you can squeeze your urethral muscle to help keep the urine in. When you're ready to empty your bladder, the brain sends signals down that relaxes a sphincter to allow you to urinate. The bladder, which is like a muscular but stretchy bag, then contracts and the urine flows out the urethra, giving you relief.

Thirsty?

Thirst is triggered by your *kidneys* and the hypothalamus in your brain. The hypothalamus checks your blood to see if it has enough water. If it does not, the hypothalamus tells your kidneys to take action! Your kidneys react by conserving water in your body. This process makes you feel thirsty, telling you to drink liquids!

Why is Urine Yellow?

The yellow color comes from the breakdown of red blood cells, which happen to turn yellow in your urine.

?

Water, please!
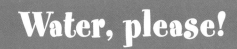

Camels can survive more than thirty days without water— no wonder they're the ideal companion for a trek through the desert. You can last only three days!

Feel the Rhythm

EVERY CELL NEEDS OXYGEN TO FUNCTION—YOUR BRAIN needs it to think, your muscles need it to move. Oxygen in the air is taken into your lungs where it's picked up by your blood. Your heart then pumps the blood all over your body, delivering the necessary oxygen to your cells to keep you alive.

Your lungs are contained by rib bones, their protective casing. When your body needs to breathe, your brain stem coordinates a contraction of your diaphragm. Your diaphragm is a large muscle beneath your lungs. When it contracts, the space for the lungs gets bigger and air rushes in through your nose and mouth and travels down your trachea and into your lungs. For you to exhale, your diaphragm relaxes and goes up, pressing on your lungs and pushing the air out.

Lung

Out of Breath?

Did you know that your body can't sense oxygen? When you try to hold your breath but you feel the need to breathe again, your body is actually telling you it senses too much carbon dioxide—rather than not enough oxygen!

?

Hard-Working Heart

**It's your heart's job to pump blood around your body.
Your heart** is made up of four chambers: two *atria* and
two *ventricles*. Your left ventricle is the strongest of
the four chambers. It has to pump blood throughout
your entire body. Your right ventricle is the second
strongest. It pumps blood to your lungs and then
back to the heart.

Can You Feel Your Aorta?

Your aorta is the biggest of all your
arteries (the tubes that carry blood away
from your heart). You may be able to feel
your heart pumping blood into your aorta
if you lie down, relax your abdominal
muscles, and press firmly
down near your belly
button.

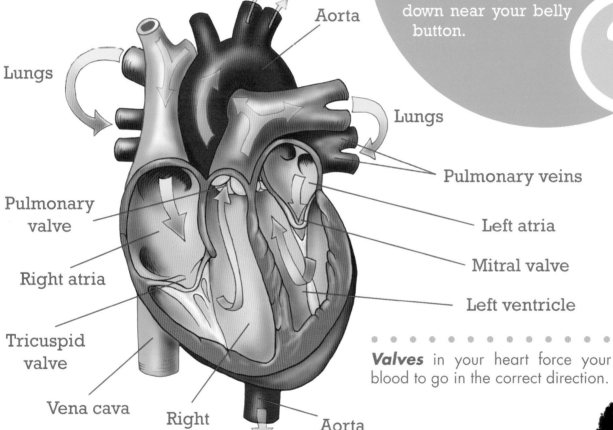

Aorta

Lungs

Lungs

Pulmonary veins

Pulmonary valve

Left atria

Mitral valve

Right atria

Left ventricle

Tricuspid valve

Vena cava

Right ventricle

Aorta

• • • • • • • • • • • • • • • • • •

Valves in your heart force your
blood to go in the correct direction.

• •

Your **HEART** is made up of a unique type of
muscle called *cardiac muscle*. Cardiac muscle cells
are linked together though electrical connections,
and when one cell contracts, all the others sense
the electricity and they contract as well.

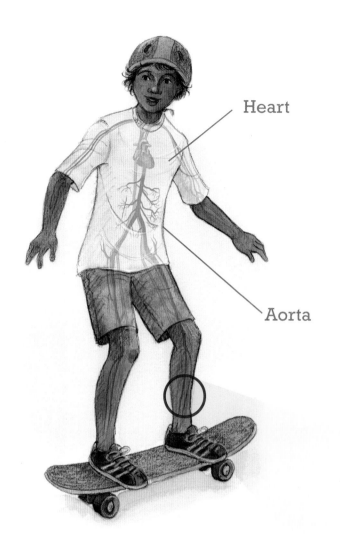

Heart

Aorta

How Does Blood Deliver Oxygen to the Organs That Need It?

Different organs need different amounts of blood at different times. When your muscles are working hard, like when you're running, the arteries leading to your leg muscles get bigger, which allows more blood to flow to them. When blood gets to an organ, the bigger vessels (arteries) divide into very small vessels called capillaries. Capillaries are so tiny, your blood cells have to travel in a single-file line to fit through them. The capillaries' small size means that your organs come in close-enough contact with your blood for oxygen to pass into them.

Once your blood is through your capillaries, it flows into larger vessels called *veins*. The veins lead back to your heart. The biggest vein is called the *vena cava*. From your heart, your blood is pumped to your lungs, where it picks up new, fresh oxygen and drops off the old carbon dioxide. Finally, your blood travels back to your left atrium and then your left ventricle, back where it started!

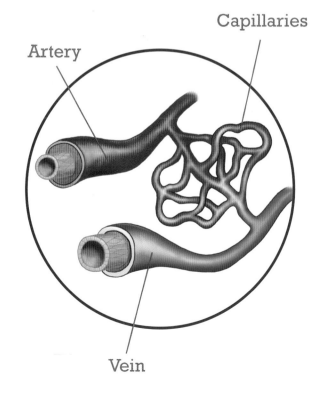

Artery

Capillaries

Vein

Listen Closely...

You can actually hear the heart's valves closing. If you put your ear to someone's chest, you hear a "lub dub" beat. Lub, the first sound, happens when the *mitral* and *tricuspid* valves close. Dub, the second sound, happens when the *aortic* and *pulmonary* valves close.

When you decide to kick a soccer ball, you don't have to tell your *quadricep*, *tibialis anterior*, and *psoas* muscles to contract, but that's what your brain does. Your brain automatically sends signals to the appropriate muscles, telling them to contract and perform complex actions. The more you practice a motion, the better you will be at performing it.

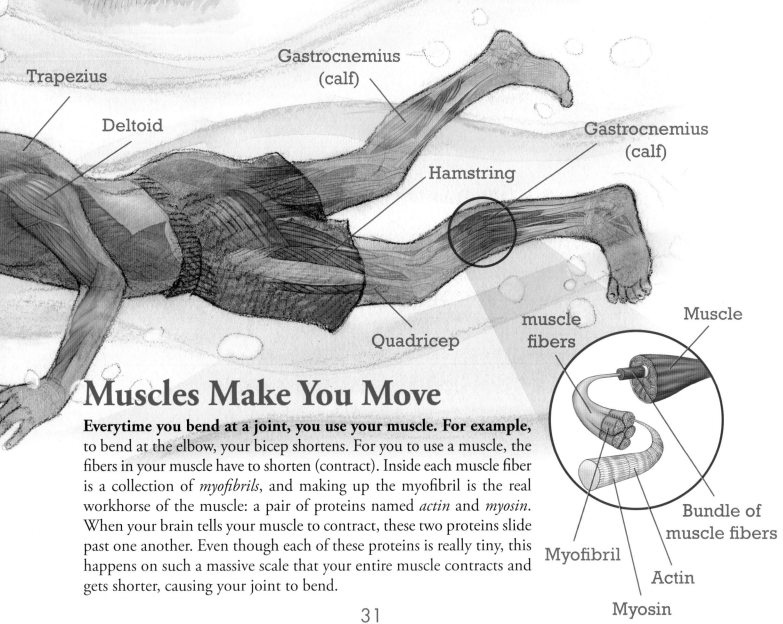

Trapezius

Deltoid

Gastrocnemius (calf)

Gastrocnemius (calf)

Hamstring

Quadricep

muscle fibers

Muscle

Myofibril

Actin

Myosin

Bundle of muscle fibers

Muscles Make You Move

Everytime you bend at a joint, you use your muscle. For example, to bend at the elbow, your bicep shortens. For you to use a muscle, the fibers in your muscle have to shorten (contract). Inside each muscle fiber is a collection of *myofibrils*, and making up the myofibril is the real workhorse of the muscle: a pair of proteins named *actin* and *myosin*. When your brain tells your muscle to contract, these two proteins slide past one another. Even though each of these proteins is really tiny, this happens on such a massive scale that your entire muscle contracts and gets shorter, causing your joint to bend.

31

Down to the Bone

WITHOUT BONES, WE WOULD JUST BE BAGS OF GOOP. But bones provide more than just structural support, they also protect your most vital organs, like your heart and lungs. Bones are alive and are always changing. They're not the dried, dead things you see in a classroom. In fact, bones contain bone marrow, which is where all of your blood cells come from.

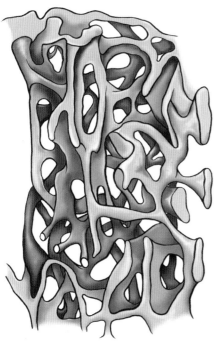

Bone Magnified

Your **BONES** are designed to be as strong as possible while still being relatively light. Bones actually have lots of tiny holes in them!

There are 206 bones in a fully grown adult. You actually had even more bones when you were born, but some of them fused together and are counted as one when you're grown up.

The biggest bone in your body is your femur, which is found in your leg, and the smallest is the stapes (stirrup) bone in your ear.

Because bones are constantly being reshaped, broken bones can heal themselves. A doctor will usually line up your bone how it was before it was broken and then leave the rest of the healing to it.

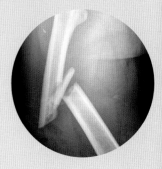

White Blood?

There are many different types of white blood cells—which are involved in fighting infections and helping to keep you healthy. If you cut yourself, lots of white blood cells go to the wound to prevent any bacteria or other invaders from getting into your body.

Why Are Veins Blue if Blood Is Red?

Your blood is actually not a red liquid. The liquid of blood (plasma) is clear yellow, and what makes your blood appear red are the red blood cells. Red blood cells' main job is to carry oxygen to the rest of the body. When red blood cells have oxygen, they look bright red. Once they have released their oxygen, they turn a deep maroon. The blood vessels you can see just under your skin are veins, which have blood that has already dropped its oxygen. The blood is really a deep maroon, but when you see it through your skin, it appears blue!

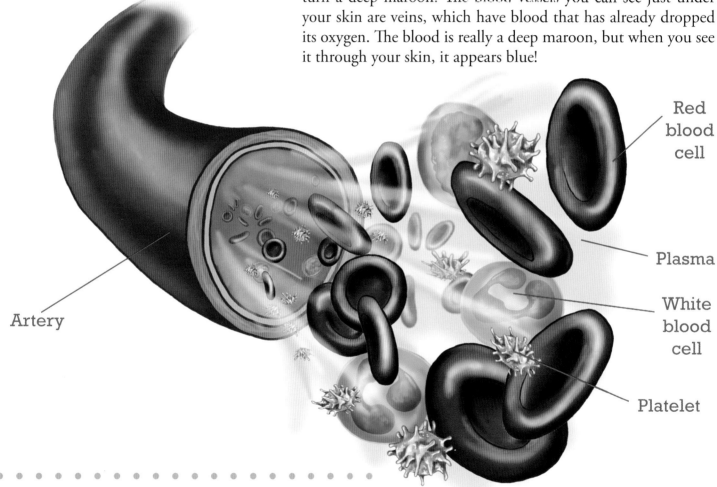

Red blood cell

Plasma

White blood cell

Platelet

Artery

PLATELETS, tiny cell fragments, help you form a blood clot, or a scab, when you cut yourself. They work together with special proteins to form web-like structures that help fix any holes and plug up the wound.

What's an "Asthma Attack?"

When your lungs are exposed to various irritants, they can swell. This causes your airways to narrow, and fill with mucus, making breathing more difficult. When a person with asthma has an attack, the tubes thicken, the airways constrict (narrow), and it becomes difficult to breathe. To fix this, a person who has asthma breathes a special medicine which causes the airways to dilate (expand) and allows him or her to breathe.

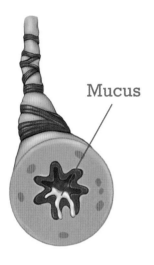

Mucus

Constricted airway

Open airway

No Smoking, Please!

If you get an **INFECTION** of the lungs, your bronchi can have a buildup of fluid and mucus. When you cough, you help expel that extra junk that has built up in your lungs.

When the cells of the lungs are exposed to smoke, several bad things can occur. Smoke can irritate the lungs, which leads to coughing and can cause an asthma attack. If the lungs are continually exposed to smoke, chemicals in the smoke can actually change the way the cells work and can turn normal, healthy cells into cancerous ones.

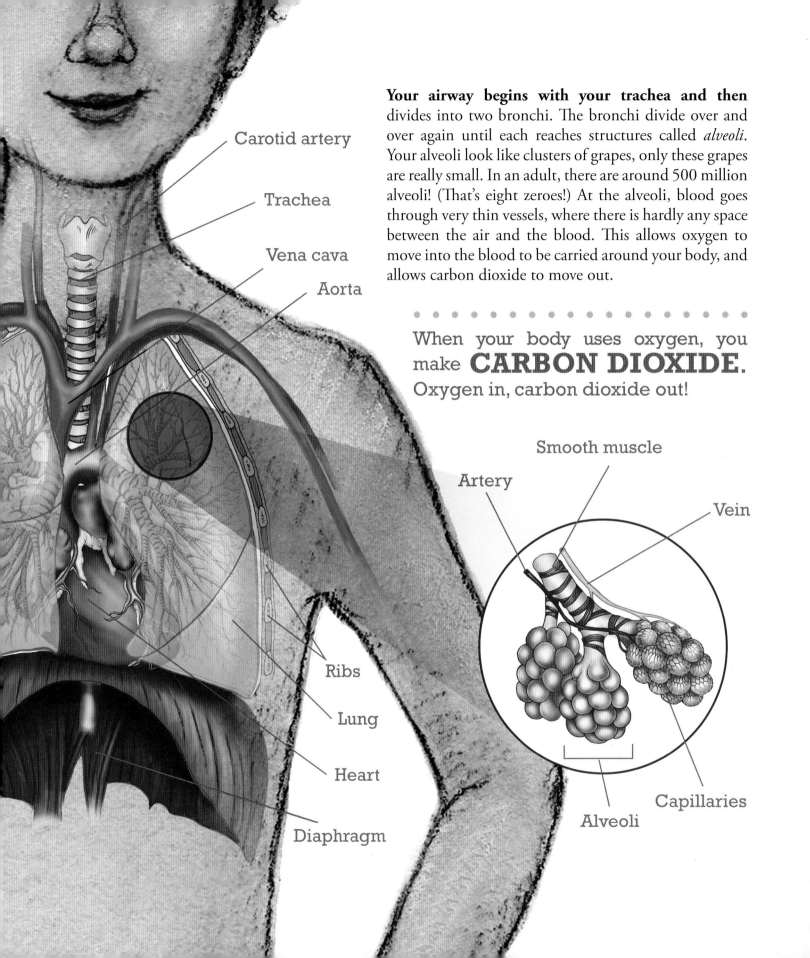

Carotid artery

Trachea

Vena cava

Aorta

Your airway begins with your trachea and then divides into two bronchi. The bronchi divide over and over again until each reaches structures called *alveoli*. Your alveoli look like clusters of grapes, only these grapes are really small. In an adult, there are around 500 million alveoli! (That's eight zeroes!) At the alveoli, blood goes through very thin vessels, where there is hardly any space between the air and the blood. This allows oxygen to move into the blood to be carried around your body, and allows carbon dioxide to move out.

. . . .

When your body uses oxygen, you make **CARBON DIOXIDE.**
Oxygen in, carbon dioxide out!

Smooth muscle

Artery

Vein

Ribs

Lung

Heart

Capillaries

Alveoli

Diaphragm

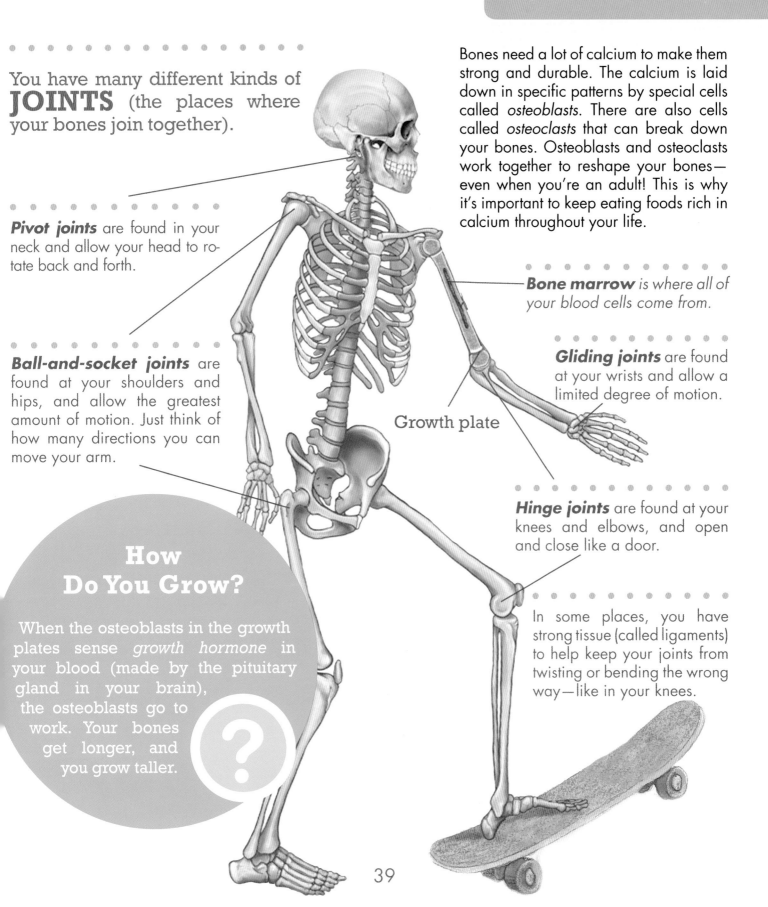

You have many different kinds of **JOINTS** (the places where your bones join together).

Bones need a lot of calcium to make them strong and durable. The calcium is laid down in specific patterns by special cells called *osteoblasts*. There are also cells called *osteoclasts* that can break down your bones. Osteoblasts and osteoclasts work together to reshape your bones—even when you're an adult! This is why it's important to keep eating foods rich in calcium throughout your life.

Pivot joints are found in your neck and allow your head to rotate back and forth.

Bone marrow is where all of your blood cells come from.

Ball-and-socket joints are found at your shoulders and hips, and allow the greatest amount of motion. Just think of how many directions you can move your arm.

Gliding joints are found at your wrists and allow a limited degree of motion.

Growth plate

How Do You Grow?

When the osteoblasts in the growth plates sense *growth hormone* in your blood (made by the pituitary gland in your brain), the osteoblasts go to work. Your bones get longer, and you grow taller.

Hinge joints are found at your knees and elbows, and open and close like a door.

In some places, you have strong tissue (called ligaments) to help keep your joints from twisting or bending the wrong way—like in your knees.

39

You're Surrounded!

Y OU ARE SURROUNDED BY GERMS ALL THE TIME! WHEN people talk about germs, they usually are referring to viruses and bacteria. Viruses and some bacteria can make you sick. This tends to happen when new, bad bacteria release toxic chemicals or when they invade places they should not go. But not all bacteria are bad. In your large intestine, bacteria live peacefully and can actually help you.

Do Not Enter!

The skin on your hands stops a lot of bacteria or viruses from entering your body, but if you get a cut or if you wipe your eyes with dirty hands, the bacteria or viruses can enter your body there. This is why it is important to clean wounds and wash your hands often.

Bacteria and viruses are very small. In fact, bacteria are the smallest living thing in the world. Viruses are even smaller, and while not technically living organisms, they can still infect you, (like when you get the flu). When a virus infects you, it turns an otherwise innocent cell into a virus-making factory that stops working for you and instead makes thousands of other viruses that can infect other cells.

To help combat these microscopic enemies, you have special immune cells located throughout your body that protect you. In your blood, these are your white blood cells. They can produce a special protein called an *antibody*. The antibody can surround and stick to viruses or bacteria, marking them for destruction. Other cells then eat the invaders.

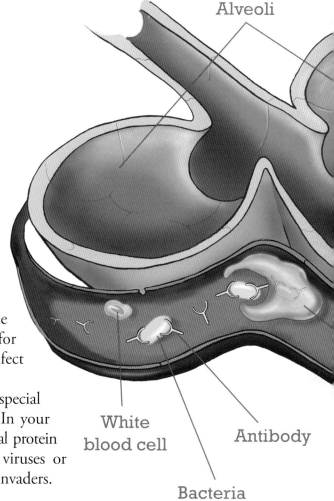

Alveoli

White blood cell

Antibody

Bacteria

Allergic Reactions

Although having a reaction to something foreign in the body is usually a good thing, sometimes your body may be overly sensitive. When you breathe in an allergen, like pollen, your body overreacts to something fairly harmless. When mast cells (a kind of white blood cell) come into contact with pollen, they release *histamine,* which tells other cells that you are under attack. Soon, your eyes begin watering, you start coughing, and your nose starts to run. Doctors can treat allergies by giving medicines that block histamine (*antihistamines*).

Why Do You Get a Rash?

When you have an allergic reaction to poison oak or poison ivy, you see a rash. A chemical attaches to your skin that confuses your white blood cells and makes them think that your skin is infected with a virus or bacteria. This causes them to start attacking your skin giving you an itchy or painful rash.

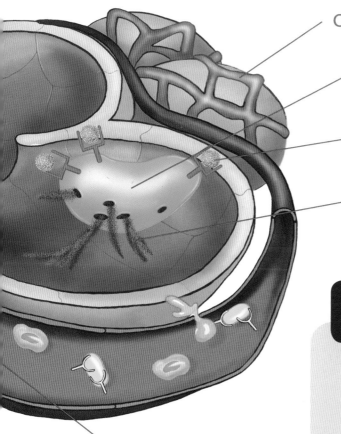

Capillary

Mast cell

Pollen

Histamine

White blood cell

Be Prepared!

When you get an immunization shot at your doctor's office, your body is exposed to a harmless version of a virus or bacteria. The immune cells learn all about how to defeat the invader, so that if you are ever exposed to the actual virus or bacteria, your body will be ready with a set of cells specially designed to get rid of that germ.

41

Send a Signal

HELPING YOUR BODY COORDINATE ALL OF ITS FUNCTIONS are hormones. Hormones are chemical signals that travel through the blood to help different organs work. They tell your body when to grow and develop. They help you compete and cope with stress. And hormones help mature bodies prepare to reproduce.

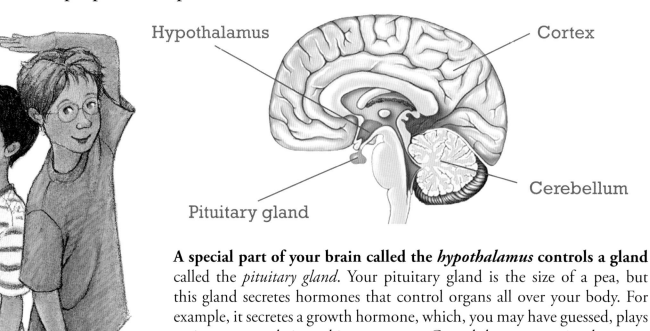

Hypothalamus

Cortex

Pituitary gland

Cerebellum

A special part of your brain called the *hypothalamus* controls a gland called the *pituitary gland*. Your pituitary gland is the size of a pea, but this gland secretes hormones that control organs all over your body. For example, it secretes a growth hormone, which, you may have guessed, plays an important role in making you grow. Growth hormones stimulate your muscles and your bones, telling the muscles to grow and get stronger and telling the bones to get longer. It also brings on puberty—when your body changes to look less like a child's and more like an adult's. Growth hormones are secreted mainly while you are asleep, so don't stay up too late!

HORMONES are also responsible for coordinating reproductive functions to prepare for and support a pregnancy. After the pregnancy is complete, hormones also help the mother make milk to feed her baby.

Sugar–Always Sweet?

Your pancreas not only aids digestion but also helps regulate the amount of sugar in your blood. Some sugar in your blood is good for you and gives your muscles and your brain the energy they need to work. But when a person is diabetic, sugar levels can be too high, and cells all over the body can be damaged, including the eyes, heart, and nerves.

Adrenal

Kidneys

Your *thyroid* produces a hormone called *thyroxine* which controls your metabolic rate (the amount of energy you use). Thyroxine causes your muscles to burn more energy and your heart to pump faster. But too much thyroxine can be dangerous, so the thyroid is carefully regulated by hormones.

Thyroid

Thyroid cartilage

Butterflies in Your Stomach!

When your body becomes stressed—when you're nervous, scared, or excited—your *adrenal gland* produces large amounts of *adrenaline*. Adrenaline is the hormone responsible for the feeling of "butterflies in your stomach" and the feeling that your heart is beating faster and stronger in your chest. Though there are not really any butterflies in your stomach, your heart does in fact beat stronger and faster in your chest when you're nervous—it's your body's way of preparing you for whatever you need to do next.

Welcome to the World!

REPRODUCTIVE ORGANS ARE SPECIALLY DESIGNED FOR making children. Unlike the other organ systems, the man's and the woman's reproductive organs are unique.

Woman

The reproductive cell of the woman is the *oocyte* (egg). These eggs are stored in the *ovaries*, which are inside the body. Starting at puberty, the ovaries prepare one egg every month for fertilization. The *fallopian tubes* connect the ovaries to the *uterus*, an organ designed to nourish a developing human. The *vagina* connects the uterus to the outside world and is the canal a fully developed baby will travel down when he or she is being born.

• • • • • • • • • • • • • •

When a woman is born, she already has all the **EGG** cells she will ever make. However, a man makes new **SPERM** throughout his life.

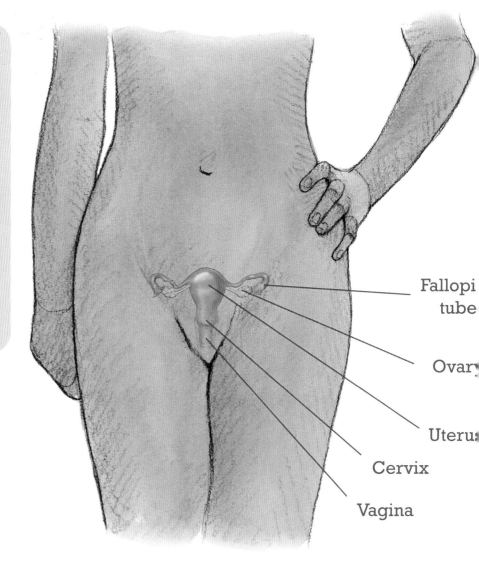

Fallopi
tube

Ovary

Uterus

Cervix

Vagina

44

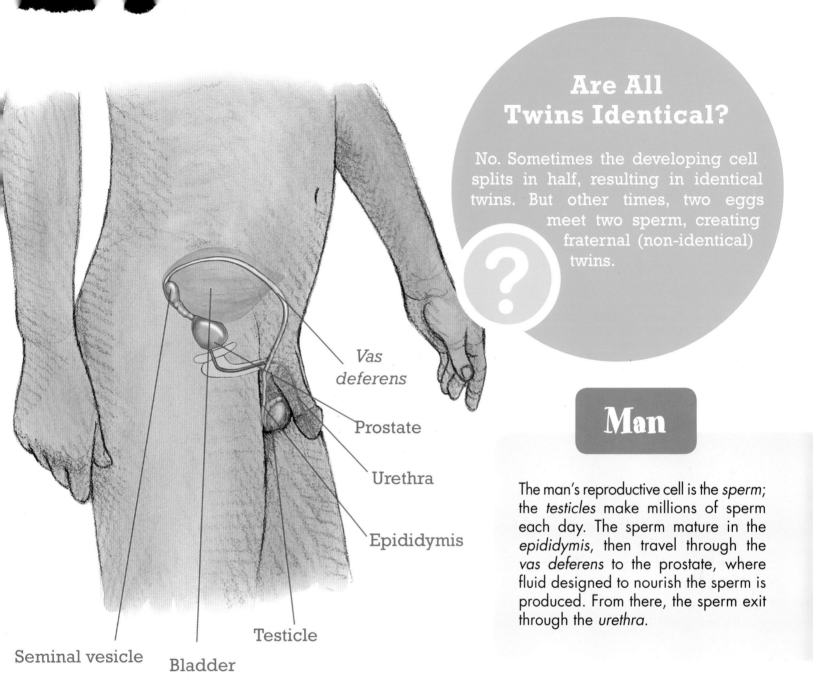

Are All Twins Identical?

No. Sometimes the developing cell splits in half, resulting in identical twins. But other times, two eggs meet two sperm, creating fraternal (non-identical) twins.

Vas deferens

Prostate

Urethra

Epididymis

Testicle

Seminal vesicle

Bladder

Man

The man's reproductive cell is the *sperm*; the *testicles* make millions of sperm each day. The sperm mature in the *epididymis*, then travel through the *vas deferens* to the prostate, where fluid designed to nourish the sperm is produced. From there, the sperm exit through the *urethra*.

You are Half Mom and Half Dad

When a sperm and egg meet, they become a single cell—sharing genetic information from both the mother and the father. That single cell grows and divides multiple times and comes to rest in the uterus. As it divides, the cells begin to become more specialized and start to make up each organ system you have already learned about.

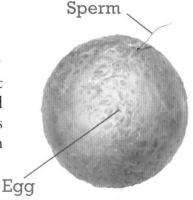

Sperm

Egg

47

Innie or Outie?

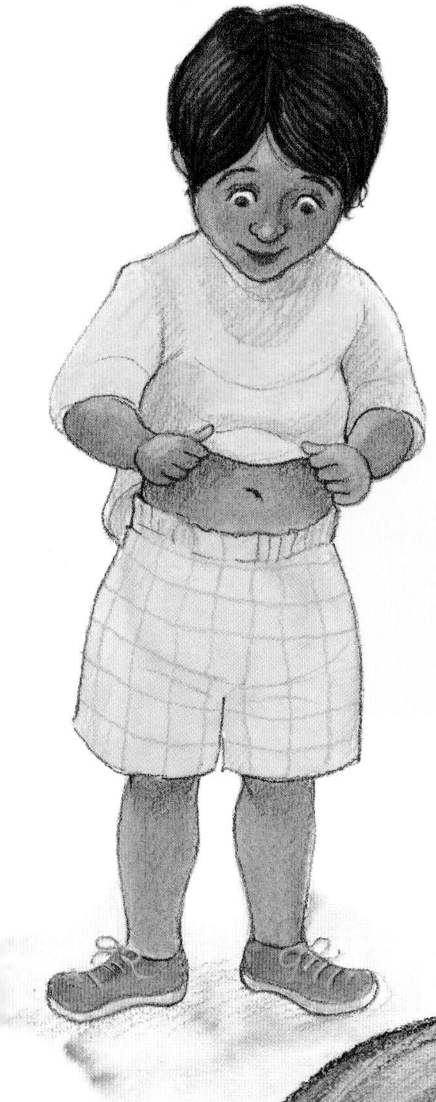

After you are born, the umbilical cord is tied off and cut. As you grow, that stump of tissue becomes the belly button.

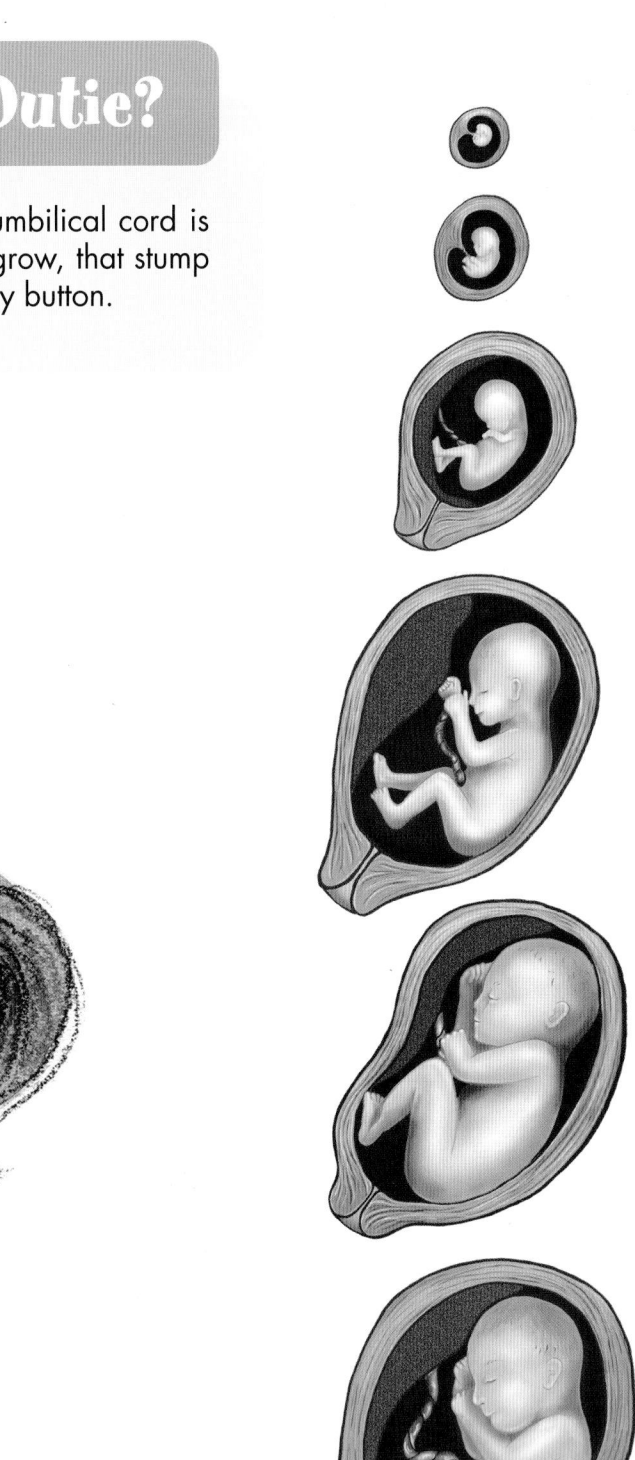

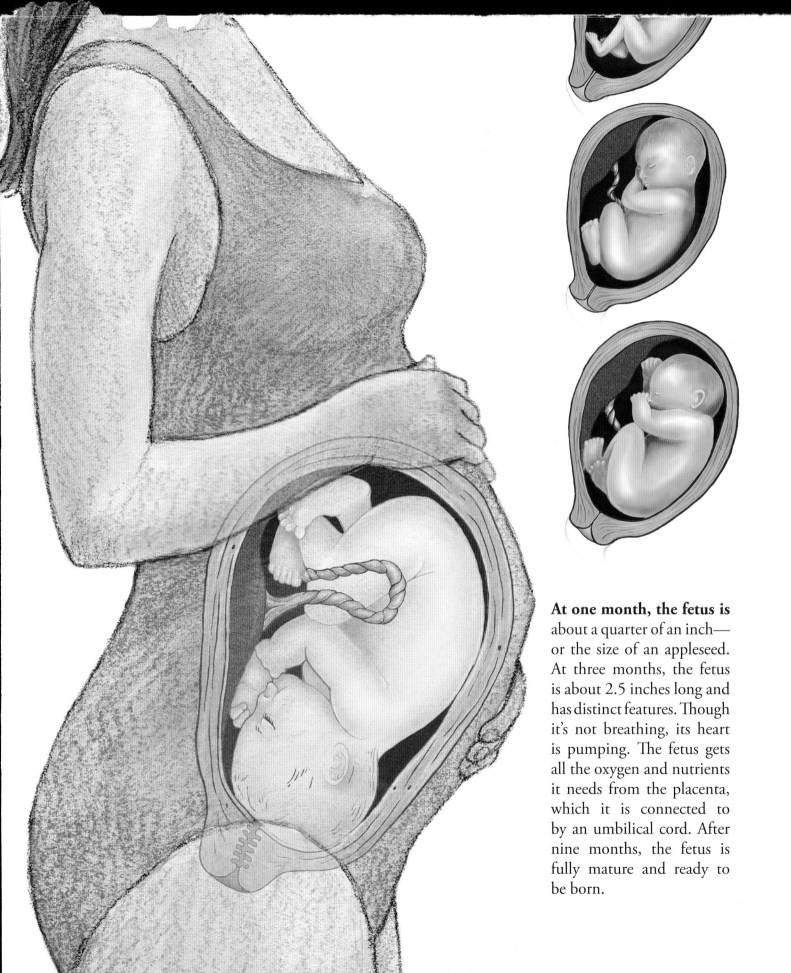

At one month, the fetus is about a quarter of an inch—or the size of an appleseed. At three months, the fetus is about 2.5 inches long and has distinct features. Though it's not breathing, its heart is pumping. The fetus gets all the oxygen and nutrients it needs from the placenta, which it is connected to by an umbilical cord. After nine months, the fetus is fully mature and ready to be born.

Words To Know

adrenaline: a hormone the body produces in response to stress.

anatomy: the scientific study of the body.

aorta: The largest artery in your body—it goes up from your heart, down through your chest, and into your abdomen.

appendix: an unnecessary structure in humans, which can occasionally become blocked and infected, requiring surgical removal.

arrector pili: a muscle that contracts when you get cold—causing goose bumps.

artery: a blood vessel that carries blood away from your heart.

bacteria: small organisms that can infect the body and release toxins.

bone: a hard tissue that provides structure and support for the body.

capillary: a small, thin blood vessel.

cell: the basic unit (building material) of all living things' central nervous system—the brain and spinal cord, which send and receive signals from all of the nerves in the body.

chromosomes: X-shaped structures in the cell—they carry genetic instructions.

cones and rods: specialized cells that sense light and send signals to nerves, allowing for sight.

Deoxyribonucleic acid: DNA, the chemical that carries genes (your genetic information), determining which characteristics you inherit from your mother and father.

digestive tract: a set of organs designed to break food down into its simplest parts, absorb nutrients into the body, and eliminate any leftover waste.

fetus: the offspring developing in the uterus after the first eight weeks.

genes: instructions found in DNA that tell the body how to develop and maintain itself.

hormones: signals that coordinate essential functions such as growth, energy use, or reproduction.

mucus: a slimy substance that serves to moisten and protect parts of the body (such as the airways inside the nose).

muscle: either cardiac, smooth, or skeletal. All muscle is capable of contracting. You can control skeletal muscles, but cardiac and smooth respond to signals beyond conscious control.

nephron: small structures in the kidney that filter blood.

organ: a distinct structure in the body that has a unique function—such as the heart, brain, or kidney.

peripheral nervous system: all of the nerves in the body, extending from and leading to the spinal cord and the brain.

peristalsis: a wave-like contraction designed to move a substance (such as food) down a tube-like organ (such as the intestine).

plasma: the watery, liquid part of blood that all the other parts of the blood float in.

reflex: an automatic, unconscious reaction.

saliva: a watery substance that helps start the digestion of food and washes your teeth.

valve: a fold or flap that allows substances to pass in one direction only.

vein: a blood vessel that carries blood back to the heart.

vena cava: the largest vein in the body. It drains into the right atrium of the heart.

villi (and microvilli): tiny structures in the intestine that allow the intestine to have extra contact with food.

Bibliography

Clemente, Carmine D. *Clemente Anatomy, a Regional Atlas of the Human Body 4th edition.* Lippincott Williams and Wilkins, 1997. ISBN: 0683303058

Costanzo, Linda S. *Physiology 4th Edition.* Lippincott Williams and Wilkins, 2007. ISBN: 0781773113

Kumar, Vinay, Ramzi S. Cotran, and Stanley L. Robbins. *Basic Pathology 7th Edition.* W.B. Saunders Company, 2003. ISBN: 0721692745

Find Out More

The Way We Work.
David Macaulay (New York: Houghton Mifflin/Walter Lorraine Books, 2008).

The Great Brain Book: An Inside Look At The Inside Of Your Head.
H.P. Newquist. Illustrated by Keith Kasnot and Eric Brace
(New York: Scholastic Reference, 2005).

My Bodyworks: Songs About Your Bones, Muscles, Heart And More!
Jane Schoenberg. Music by Steven Schoenberg. Illustrated by Cynthia Fisher
(Northhampton, MA: Crocodile Books, 2005).

Dr. Frankenstein's Human Body Book.
Richard Walker (New York: DK Publishing, 2008).

Index